CAMEOS *of* FAITH

CAMEOS of FAITH

A Collection of Theological Reflections

TODDY HOARE

RESOURCE *Publications* · Eugene, Oregon

CAMEOS OF FAITH
A Collection of Theological Reflections

Copyright © 2022 Toddy Hoare. All rights reserved. Except for brief quotations in critical publications or reviews, no part of this book may be reproduced in any manner without prior written permission from the publisher. Write: Permissions, Wipf and Stock Publishers, 199 W. 8th Ave., Suite 3, Eugene, OR 97401.

Resource Publications
An Imprint of Wipf and Stock Publishers
199 W. 8th Ave., Suite 3
Eugene, OR 97401

www.wipfandstock.com

PAPERBACK ISBN: 978-1-6667-4334-0
HARDCOVER ISBN: 978-1-6667-4335-7
EBOOK ISBN: 978-1-6667-4336-4

APRIL 29, 2022 10:38 AM

For all the recipients of some or all of my weekly Out & About collections while housebound during COVID-19 lockdown and pour encourager les autres.

Contents

List of Illustrations | vii

Preface | viii

Spiritual Reflection

Gratitude | 3

Pentecost | 4

Protestant Roots | 5

The Greeks and Romans Prayed | 6

Spiritual Reflection | 7

Navigation | 8

Pre-Testament | 9

Placing The Gods | 10

Spirituality of Ageing | 11

Stabat Mater | 12

John the Baptist | 13

Mary Magdalen | 14

Aelred | 15

Friendship | 16

Jeremiah | 17

St Cuthbert | 20

St Francis | 21

We Call It The Trinity | 22

Grief | 23

Pain | 24
A Reply to Robert Ford | 25
Reclaiming Space | 26
Musing on Death | 27
Suicide of a Neighbor | 28
Song of Songs (Sense into non-sense. MP.) | 29

8 Sonnets on My Sculpture on Exhibition at St John's College, Oxford. March 2018.

Talking Heads. Real, Ordained and Abstract. | 33
Considering the Nude | 34
Lacrimosa | 35
Jacob Wrestling | 36
John 8, vv1–12. | 37
Catwalk | 38
With Child | 39
Lord of the Dance | 40

Matters Spiritual

A Prayer for Lent & Easter | 43
At the Empty Tomb | 44
Hide & Seek. Revelation by Degrees. | 45
Resurrection | 46
It's Christmas. (A Prayer.) | 47
2015 Christmas Thoughts | 48
Christmas Cheer, Past Christmas Blackmail | 49
Magi | 51
Brangwin at Taomina | 53
Contemplating Monastic Life | 54

St Enodoc | 55

Blackfriars. Sunday after Week of Prayer. | 56

St Brides. | 57

St Brides Sermon. | 58

Llantony Abbey. | 59

Armageddon: BC 1457–AD 1918 | 60

Armistice Centenary | 61

Wisdom | 62

Pull to God | 63

Birth of the Word | 64

Christmas Card | 65

Fourthoughts of Kells | 66

Cuddesdon | 67

Vocation | 68

Winding Stair to the Pulpit. | 69

Dreaming & Sleeping | 70

Human Business | 71

Out in the World

Fake News I | 75

Fake News II | 76

US Values | 77

Better Values | 78

REFLECTIONS ON BIBLE PASSAGES

Psalms 8, 144, 80, 122 | 81

Patterns for Prayer | 82

A Word in Time | 83

John 1, v5. | 84

Lazarus, the Disciple whom Jesus Loved. | 85

To The Children of This Age. | 86

Salome's Dance | 87

A Thought for Christmas | 88

Who Is God? | 89

City Walls Abound | 90

A Wedding Poem | 91

Valuing | 92

The Comforter | 93

Catholic & Protestant Perceptions | 94

The New Israel | 95

2 Trees | 96

The Colt, the Foal of an Ass, Important on Palm Sunday | 97

Flip Sides of Nativity and Crucifixion | 98

The Good Shepherd | 99

Transfiguration | 100

Eve | 101

Climate Change and Worse | 102

Ash Wednesday 2021. | 103

Deception | 104

People | 105

Creation | 106

The Cup of Blessing. Wrath's Conversion. | 107

St. David | 108

Ruth | 109

Bathsheba | 110

St. JH Newman | 111

Blind Bartimaeus | 112

St. Patrick | 113

Grief; His on Thursday, Hers on Friday | 114

The Call of the Disciples. James. | 115
St. Thomas Misses Out | 116
St. Jude | 117
St. Matthew | 118
St.s Peter and Andrew. | 119
The Nativity. | 120

Creation

Creation. | 123
Prayer and the Environment. | 124
Evolution. Fall of a Sparrow. | 125
Hares | 126
Sparrow Hawk | 128
Curlew | 129
Owl | 130
Woodpecker, or Yaffle. | 132
Geese. | 133
Dandelion | 134
Haze of Sloes. | 135
More Dog Walking. | 136
Ode to Dogs | 137
Dog Walk Down the Lane. Walking in the Wood. | 138
Garden Outside the Window. | 139
Dawn Breaks through the Bedroom Window or The Cuckoo. | 140
Storm Ophelia. | 141
30/11/17 | 142
Ploughing With Horses. | 143
Stolen Moments | 144
To the Beloved | 145

Another Rose | 146

Family Year | 147

Patience. | 148

Cornwall Surfers. Holiday Time. | 149

Daymer Bay | 150

2018 Hogmanay Hangover | 151

Indignities | 152

Models & Miniatures | 153

Leeds Sculptures | 154

November. | 155

Senior Citizen | 156

Take on Retirement | 157

Gravity | 158

Brexit | 159

Game Shooting for the Pot | 160

Greedy Guns, or Greedy Shooting Lacking Grace. | 161

Beethoven & TS Eliot Quartets. | 162

Syncopated Sound | 163

Macbeth & Ambiguity | 164

Livery Dinners | 165

A Place of Prayer | 166

On suffering and The Lord's Prayer. | 167

Dawn, Triumph of Light | 168

The True Vineyard, Vines and Vinedresser. | 169

Art & Modernity. | 170

List of Illustrations

Mary Magdalen, 1st Apostle. Sculpture TH. Photo TH

Rapid Assessment Unit, JR hospital, Oxford. TH drawing

Seated Nude Study. Drawing TH

Lacrimosa, Head TH. Photo TH

Jacob Wrestling. Genesis 32. Bronze, TH

Woman Taken in Adultery, John 8. Bronze relief, TH

Catwalk, a take on fashion by TH. Photo TH

With Child. Bronze, TH

Lord of the Dance. Bronze. TH

The Good Shepherd. John 10; Psalm 23. Bronze TH

Ruth or Humility. Bronze, TH

St. John Henry Newman, roundel. Bronze, TH

Blind Bartimaeus. Bronze, TH

Hare Trinity. Drawing TH

Hares Boxing. Drawing TH

Owl. Drawing TH

Owl in Flight. Linocut print, TH

Cassandra. Sketch for sculpture reliefs, Stations of the Odyssey. TH

Plough Sunday. Parish Magazine cover sketch TH

Felix and Pedal Car. Watercolour TH

Portrait Study. TH

Macbeth, Open Air performance at Lady Margaret Hall, Oxford. Pen sketch, TH

Preface

THESE POEMS WERE WRITTEN to lift the spirits in darker times with various themes and reflections based on matters spiritual, my sculpture, creation, and observations of life in general, along with reflections on past experiences. One of the beauties of poetry is that less is more and one can leave the reader with far more than a few lines encompass. From school days John Donne has always influenced my poetry writing along with similar content and themes which is why I stick to a loose sonnet form for conciseness and a final punch in the last two lines.

I have found that often composing and writing a poem differs little from expressing thoughts in prayer and therefore becoming a prayer for others when leading worship and drawing on the more familiar. Thus the Beatitudes, Matt. 5, vv. 1-11:

> Heavenly Father may we know our needs and enter your kingdom.
> May we bring comfort to the needy.
> May our meekness win the earth,
> May our desire and longing for righteousness prevail.
> To encourage mercy help us to show mercy.
> In the purity of our hearts may we see you.
> Help us to promote peace in your Son's name.
> Help us to take the rough with the smooth,
> And to be an example of the inheritance you give us,
> That we may further your Kingdom in your Son's name. Amen.

On the other hand the poem poses pause for prayer or deeper reflection or a journey into mindfulness.

The illustrations, sculpture and photography are entirely my own to further brighten up people's thoughts.

Lastly I must add words of thanks. Having made an application for a grant from the Arts Council UK to cover my production contribution I would like to thank their support team for their patience and help in guiding me through the labyrinth of the submission form. Heartfelt thanks go to Ben Jeapes for preparing my manuscript to Wipf and Stock specification and relieving me of fumbling with skills I do not have! Special thanks must

Preface

go to Matthew Wimer for the confidence to take on the publishing of this volume which is a great encouragement to me. No words of thanks would be complete without loving thanks to Liz whose vocation to Wycliffe Hall has given me the freedom to be, doing sculpture and returning to writing, after 25 years of enjoyable parish ministry in North Yorkshire.

—T. H. Holton, Oxford, March 2022.

Spiritual Reflection

GRATITUDE

The Lord's Prayer urges all to say
All things we need each day,
Indeed demand rather than pray;
What room for thanks called to obey?
If we show God no gratitude
Do we live out some platitude?
Mindful of each beatitude
Are these a thankful attitude?
Politeness dictates that thanks shown
Reflect an appreciation grown;
Another's actions we don't disown,
Become a seed of friendship sown.
Of each little deed recognition
Is sure sign of valuation
Or of difference a resolution
Generating this flutter of emotion.
God centered life is grateful reply
If on obedience and forgiveness we rely.

PENTECOST

What were those tongues of flame like fire
That descended from way above?
Perhaps a flickering Holy Dove
Changing overhead auras of the crowd
Enabling talk in divers languages out loud;
Holy Spirit will others inspire.
This heavenly fiery sign of power
Energizes open minds to fresh
Wisdom giving all a context
Where Jesus lives in each. There follows next
Peace that passes all understanding. Flesh
Contains strength like the psalmist's tower.
Communication of Good News knows
No bounds as Holy Spirit's grace flows.

PROTESTANT ROOTS

Oxford Schools Hensley Henson lecture
Thomas Cromwell was the subject
Diarmaid MacCulloch erudite speaker
Having researched contemporary correspondence
Giving us quotes, of nuggets a preponderance.
The course of Protestantism established
Popish practices were gradually banished
And how Catholic influence grew weaker
So what he said was no conjecture
Instead amazing far from abject;
How Swiss style foundations were laid
Men neither Cardinal nor King obeyed;
This layman's hidden legacy was brought to view
To which the Church of England remains true.

THE GREEKS AND ROMANS PRAYED

Here are folk who prayed to God
(Calling him Zeus) and to lesser gods
For success tempting fate.
Dwelling on God their anxieties
Over lesser gods led to failure
In their quests, for sacrifices
Seen as service not risk courage
Boosted. Prayer and libation
Contained a tenderness and peace,
A restful heart, but petition
Could include serious sedition
Much like later Romans to Jove.
Prayer is little changed save the focus
On God as made known to us.

SPIRITUAL REFLECTION

Disconnected, the mind needs space
To find equilibrium. Reflection
Leads to Inner calm and peace
Offering confidence and reconciliation
By reviewing faith and identity.
Who am I, where am I going, what are my strengths?
Confronting self opens, removes pity,
Truth has power to rightfully predict
Able to face those who go to any lengths
To confound, confuse and contradict
Raising the individual above rejection.
Experiencing all humiliation
Jesus man's spiritual depths plumbed
That individuals to no worse succumbed.

NAVIGATION

Until the Moral compass unrefined
Is properly swung personality
Runs aground, remains undefined
Disconnected from self, a liability,
Lacking light to see light. Forward going,
Reflecting spiritually is to stand back
Assessing what personality may lack
To restore inner confidence self-knowing.
Respect won dissent resolved
Peace restored where values involved,
Channeled past rock of belligerency
And hard place of obstinacy.

PRE-TESTAMENT

Gods of Greek myths were located
in prominent positions
to adopt the land as residents
outlook of new settlements
master traders remains dated
long before monotheism expands
temples make complex rows reaching
shadows of fading wealth, suspicions,
power passing into other hands
theaters and arenas stressed
values, culture, communal teaching.
Roman life differently expressed
then former Sea Peoples expels
save their costly purple dyes from shells.

PLACING THE GODS

Darling daughter deprived Demeter,
Darkness descending, future stoney,
Lamented stolen Persephone,
Like Eve apple bearer but not eater,
Though robbed save lust for no reason
Bringing to dust that mourning Season
When nature shrinks. Effort is needed
To prepare for next year's glories
Ere all is choked unless weeded.
Such cycles described by stories
Winter sweetened by summer's honey
Not all explanations are funny
Anticipating her return from another
Restoring fertility to earth child to mother.

SPIRITUALITY OF AGEING

As I grow older I gain greater freedom
By shedding what I cannot do nor achieve
Yet simultaneously more captive I become
To corporal restrictions while I believe
Ultimate liberty comes with death.
Each day an adventure while I have breath.
Ever busy when things take longer
There is time to read and ponder,
Write up thoughts, scan an idea
Support the family in prayer . . .
Can carry dog biscuits by the bag;
Yet fingers turn pages with painful jag.
Hands still work clay but not what's so fiddly
Eyes misjudge pouring drink before I'm tiddly.

STABAT MATER

> It was remarked there was a shortage of
> a contemporary look at a classic theme.

There stands his mother, hesitant, short of breath,
Supported afar off in her anguish by others
As her son, who once snoozed upon her breast
When a babe taking a nourished rest,
Now dies a lingering terrorist's death,
That they in turn mete out, vile brothers,
To those of a different persuasion.
His crucified body on his deposition
Will have a final maternal embrace
With kisses on his disfigured face
Actions as sharp as piercing sword.
Your grief is ours for one adored.
Where in such sorrow can grace reside
Escaping death's dominion that love abide?

JOHN THE BAPTIST

Repent, repent, the Kingdom's nigh
Turn back to your Lord on high.
Re-enter now the Promised Land
Receive those Blessings freely given
Salvation of souls is now at hand.
Serve God alone with conscience clear
Washing off all sin in Jordan River.
Soon will come the Spirit giver
Power from high to daunt all fear.
Come too the Kingdom of Heaven
Where God's will is done by all
Restoring the children of the fall.
Thus John the Baptist launched the way
That none from God might further stray.

MARY MAGDALEN

> When the study of Mary Magdalene as the First Apostle appeared in *The Times* it caused a flurry of letters disputing and supporting the title I gave it in the light of my reading the facts in the Gospels.

Many Marys made their mark
Not least the Magdalen, maid
Maybe mother, exposed and stark,
Sicut Lilium, recognition made
The garden of sorrows a delight,
Though Mark records they ran in fright,
To find her Lord restored for evermore.
Commissioned apostle news to tell
She has witnessed that all is well,
No need to go to Galilee shore.
Of her past there's so little we know
Save that she was a lady of means
Following the Lord where he might go
Supplying more than empty dreams.
Seven devils – who knows what kind?
Mary Magdalen restored in mind.

AELRED*

What can be more valuable than a friend?
To spurn friendship is to blot out the sun.
Where two or three gather in God's name
Then He's of the group to seal the same
In a bond that death can't leave undone.
Friendship endures all to the very end.
Abiding in love God is friendship living
A friend is the best medicine every season
Yet one must know the other
If better honored without bother,
Governed by justice, honor and reason
To be sacramental, self-giving.
Extending friendship is warming to charm
Praying those close come to no harm.

* 3rd Abbot of Rievaulx, 1147-67, aged 57.

FRIENDSHIP*

What is more valuable than a friend?
Spurned friendship's like blotting out the sun.
Where 2 or 3 are gathered in his name
There He is to seal the same
In a bond that cannot be undone
For friendship endures to the very end.
A friend is the best medicine
Yet one must honor the other;
Friendship is warming to another's charm
Praying those close meet no harm,
Giving greater honor without rancor.
Abiding in love is abiding in God. Begin
Governed by reason, honor and justice,
Sacramental, self-giving, demanding no price.

---

* Fr Aelred wrote 'Spiritual Friendship'.

JEREMIAH

1. The Prophet

The Holy Spirit was upon me from an early age
Binding me to prophesy uttering God's word.
People ask "What is the burden of the Lord?"
Thinking it weighs me down, in turn
Restricting them who are the burden of the Lord.
They reject his provision, refuse to learn.
My actions are illustrations in temple and town,
Artist and priest open to serve God alone.
I speak as God says not babble for a wage.
Like a prostitute the many lovers Judah savors,
Profanes her faith with fornication cruder
By admitting other gods to her favors.
'Repent, return, leave the Ark of Covenant alone,
For Jerusalem is my dwelling and my throne.'

2. Symbols

I watch the almond tree for early signs;
A smoking pot gives north direction;
Israel prefers broken cisterns to Living Water's flow.
Spared Egyptian service no thanks you show
By serving God, exhibit no discretion
Turning to other gods in red light lines.
'My sun-like anger parches land; you'll find
Water and wells drying up de-hydrating stock.
You forfeit my care, handmade idols no help yield
Doing less for you than scarecrows in a field.
I chose you but your abominations mock;
Child sacrifice never crossed my mind.'
Expensive linen pants hid in a watery cleft
Rot, highlighting in Israel what little worth is left.

3. Jeremiah speaks as God told him

'Your welfare will be what you seek, spared violation,
In foreign lands.' Like a potter discards
Malformed work so I consign you to learn
A hard lesson before regaining what you yearn.
The purchased flask is shattered into shards
To mirror in Babylon your desolation.
'I promise a good shepherd to tend my flock.
You'll return like a basket of choice figs proffered
After you drink up the cup of my wrath.
Accept my yoke lest one like iron from the north,
More harsh, will replace your rebellion. I offered
Salvation if you became purified stock.
I cut a new covenant of restoration,
Of temple worship and a mighty nation.'

4. More prophetic action

In Anathoth I bought my cousin's land;
In time transactions would be resuming.
The nobles reneged the six year rule as neighbors
Releasing Hebrew slaves from forced labors.
The priests imprisoned me presuming
To prophesy what God rejected out of hand.
The Rechabites were faithful to their heritage
Promising no strong drink when tested.
I was cast in a cistern full of mire,
Rescued by Ebed-melech as my fate was dire,
Rationed on royal command but house arrested.
Jehoiakim burnt Baruch's scribed scroll page by page.
Then Zedekiah rebelled so worse befell,
Blinded by Nebuchadnezzar when Jerusalem fell.

5. Finally, post Cachemish

With exile ensued murder, intrigue, herded like cattle
From wasted Judah, temple trampled, walls felled.
My guardian Gedaliah assassinated. Then
Despite I warned of false sanctuary when
To Egypt I was assigned, against my will held,
To fall under foreign rule with defeat in battle.
I prophesied yet further fate that nations
Would be treated as they had treated God's elect,
Who previously had Jerusalem bedeviled
Would be overthrown in turn and leveled,
When former Mede allies Chaldeans eject.
Israel would stay in Babylon for several generations
Exiles eking out their identity in misery
To return a remnant with new history.

ST CUTHBERT

Reflecting rotary movement as oyster catchers feed,
Sun shimmering on the surface of the sea
Surrounding Saint Cuthbert's solitary cell,
Hide-away from questioning men, close to God,
Dances where no wavelets lap shoreside,
Warming the foreshore now connecting
Island to mainland in turn still island
Twice daily come high tide.
Now a heaving sea of tourists
Disturb his Cuddy ducks and ancient peace,
More numerous than marauding Vikings
And more remote from God, yet still he speaks.
Does the lure of Cuthbert still draw
Folk to savor that spirituality so raw?

ST FRANCIS

Songbirds sing their morning tune
Owls hoot by the light of the moon
Dawn chorus through my open window
Wakes me before I'm ready to go.
What they chirp I've not a clue
Maybe just "How do you do?"
Or is it all territorial angst- er
"I'm as strong as any gangster"?
More likely it's done to impress
The ladies, announce their nests, dress
Their lives in dawn cacophony
Unmatched by any record from Sony.
Deprived of any congregation
St Francis preached with great elation.

WE CALL IT THE TRINITY

To stand before God embraces Sonship
To be told what we are by the Word
Letting Holy Spirit absorb us
Adoring the whole in worthy worship.
Thus thrice suffused like painted paper
As if colour would flush the face
We become charged with heavenly Grace.
There descends no clandestine vapor
Intoxicating the simple soul.
We may cite numbers there are none
Thereby the Trinity is undone,
There is no aspect from it we stole.
We can stand in that celestial presence
To let it permeate our every sense.

GRIEF

Is the agony of grief the greater
Because I am spared or left?
Is the pain sword thrust in Mary's heart,
Despite warning, that she and son must part?
Can greater sorrow than the cross leave one so bereft?
Yet grief, like Gethsemane, bleeds sooner or later.
Hours of vigil cause mounting tension.
Prompt denial, disbelief, generate reaction
Weighing down the weary shattered soul.
While reluctant truth accepts reality. A hole
Against increasing pain's accumulation
Opens within so life seems spent in suspension.
When heart and mind differently act
Memory accommodates the fact.

PAIN

Nothing's more wearying than pain
Throbbing, hot, spasms again n'again,
Lying listless or rotating to find
That comfortable position that eases
The limbs and calms the struggling mind
Unable to focus on what it pleases.
Time hangs heavy, yet moves apace
Hands still trace across clock's face
Exhaustion brings fleeting sleep
Lull from endless watches to keep.
Disconnected dreams are chased away
Only humor brings relief by day
Jacques Tati's clowning closely observes
Human behavior not tingling nerves.

**JR Oxford when I was in RAU, not an out of body experience!
Drawing in situ of Rapid Assessment Unit, JR. TH.**

A REPLY TO ROBERT FORD

I'm sorry you dropped your load
Scattering your parcels in the road.
Are you moving none left behind
Gathered up with better state of mind?
I remember juggling life
Trying to avoid descending strife.
Or is it all a frightful dream,
Life's awkward burdens that seem
Unbalanced and ready to topple down
Leaving you stranded in the town?
Is there no friend to share your load
To come to help to cross the road?
Is life some joker come to explode
Your balanced rhythms your highway code?
I feel I know you; awake, all is fine,
Your life's a burden, your burden's mine.
Your armful is a tale of woe:
I hope you're balanced and on the go.

RECLAIMING SPACE

                    Oxford Hollaback. Written for awareness in Oxford.

Some beast on the street harassed me
Violating my space, outfaced,
Leaving me sullied; embarrassed plea
Drew a laugh. Outpaced
No pursuit possible. Any witness
Turned away avoiding involvement.
Having no judo nor Karate fitness
Instant defense is mere lament,
Though not needed short of rape,
Robbery, and now terrorism
Through some warped religious prism
That channels lives with no escape.
While I can watch freely street performance
Why is keeping my space a difficult dance?

MUSING ON DEATH

What is death for mortals but a conveyance?
Take a new dimension, called fourth maybe,
Where we become messengers, God see,
Carrying our love in an instance.
"To see him as he is, for we (alive)
Like him shall be" to quote 1 John 3.
With instant thought sixteen we can be
Or sixty one. Might we see George Five
Face to face whose head old pennies graced?
I don't see death as darkness deep
But perpetual light, not sleep
Everlasting but a system interlaced,
Parallel without matter, increased thought
Added to that first Word that all things wrought.

SUICIDE OF A NEIGHBOR

Days elide when police asked when
Someone next door was last seen here.
Was it this or last week-end then?
How likely that he's been there?
Now all is ended. Was life vain?
We don't know your last doubts,
Rejection, agonies of the mind,
Sense of worthlessness, pain,
Depression's increasing bouts,
Precipitating such finality
To which neighbors were blind,
Leaving a shocking reality.
We make prayers that rest and peace
In the deceased's soul may increase.

SONG OF SONGS (SENSE INTO NON-SENSE. MP.)

The Song of Songs is enigmatic
Describing love's celebration,
Commitment, yearning, anticipation.
This poem encourages imitation
Their choice is their elation
Their passion for each other ecstatic.
Down the ages love remains fantastic.
Applicable to sundry variation
Too earthly for incarnation
Where mortal with divine finds inclination
Backbone not limit of a situation
For relationships are pragmatic.
Does the God whom we cannot see
Dictate our sexuality?

8 Sonnets on My Sculpture on Exhibition at St John's College, Oxford. March 2018.

TALKING HEADS. REAL, ORDAINED AND ABSTRACT.

When Peter Ustinov sat tales were anecdotal.
With Robbie Wraith sightings were reciprocal.
Lionel Blue to his audience was vocal.
Eve Fairfax on Rodin was historical.
Jean, an accompanist, was musical.
Theresa as Lachrymose is seen hysterical.
For the soldier No glory in war is final.
Diarmaid gives a commentary that is factual.
David Jenkins was intellectual.
A self portrait can only be visual.
Roly the clown is representational.
John Henry Newman is Cardinal.
Model for Mary Magdalen is beautiful.
A conversation piece can only be virtual.

CONSIDERING THE NUDE

The nudes are drawn (not to look forlorn)
Studies from life for curves and proportion
Becoming subjects of the artist's mind
Not for their breasts but as you find:
Bathsheba bath bound as David found.
Mary Magdalen in the round.
Aerobics appearing all contortion.
Pregnancy with child yet unborn.
Stretching, walking, reading, kneeling exercises.
Salome dances, Mary grieves, Jacob agonizes.
In contrast to Mammon's seduction
An adulteress is spared stoney destruction.
After serial temptresses lure Odysseus
Clothed Nausicaa puts his story to better use.

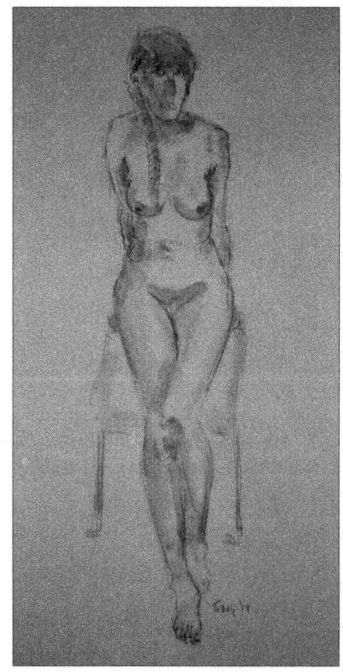

Drawing.

LACRIMOSA

Full of tears since that day a mortar took him away.
What can restore life beyond the grave?
What of the person who caused the death
Will guilt remain if none forgave?
Of one you loved, who stifled his breath
What can arise from ash or clay?
Will pardon enable victim to meet
The perpetrator face to face
In a new dimension on neutral ground?
What triumph of grace makes unbound
The agonized soul you would embrace?
Through prayer will friend and foe greet?
Asking forgiveness like the best
Grants all peace of mind, eternal rest.

Photo of Head, bronze.

JACOB WRESTLING

Jacob wrestled with his conscience and the Word of God,
Forced to face himself he found himself lacking
He needed to reform, favourite of mother.
A rotten cheat who usurped his brother
Whom he feared to encounter next day
Having sent family and flocks safely away:
Esau might even send him packing
Unlikely to return a brotherly nod.
He crossed the Jabbok, running water, inference
Of the waters of Baptism, called by a new name,
Israel, he walked with limping difference,
Relationships with Self, God and Brother not the same.
Jacob is born again spiritually complete
Renewed inner confidence whoever he might meet.

Jacob wrestling, Genesis 32. Bronze.

JOHN 8, VV 1-12.

Caught in the very act they claimed
Voyeurs, they must have lain in wait.
Why stone her without including him?
She despatched he not even named.
Was this justice or a convenient bait
To catch out a Rabbi with their whim?
"It is written" he wrote in the dust.
What?! He countered their blood-lust.
'Let him without sin cast the first stone."
One by one they melt away frightened
Weary of blood-guilt. Their noose tightened
Round their own necks. So left alone
Jesus charged her to sin no more,
Find inner peace, saved by the Law.

Woman Taken in Adultery, bronze relief.

CATWALK

Designer stuff she struts along the catwalk
Unrealistic for everyday wear
Attracts attention amongst rag-traders
With designs to rival space invaders
Convincing punters fashion's dear
Precocious style fuels talk
By columnists of what's the rage.
Millinery boasts a nude in a hat;
Military is the cut for the season
Quite bizarre with no reason
See-through, exposed thigh for all that,
Retro tweed from a bygone age.
Girls fluffed to flounce, no breasts to bounce,
What buyer for such stuff will pounce?

Catwalk. Bronze.

WITH CHILD

One stands easing the strain of frontal fulness
Energy metabolized programmed to nurture
The child within, which soon will feed,
Mother's breasts swollen to meet need
To suckle, to contentment an overture;
Sleep comes mouth feeling full, not restless,
Leaving years of a falling sensation
From being laid down. Maternal care
Supports shy toddler unsure of play.
Were these Jerusalem women on the way
To Golgotha whom Jesus addressed aware
Of his past and present destination?
Denied such peace as on a mother's breast
Till with death he enters God promised rest.

With Child, bronze.

LORD OF THE DANCE

Integral circle of apostles rotate
Round Trinity contra-rotating
Inward focused faith promoting
Throng of people not closed gate
Capable of opening to accept
Newcomers ever on their way.
Solid standing stones state their claim
Their meaning lost while they remain
Welcoming people in their day
Guarding the rituals they kept.
Church today is not that static
But could be much more elastic
Temptation is to be exclusive
When attitudes should be inclusive.

Lord of the Dance. Bronze.

Matters Spiritual

A PRAYER FOR LENT & EASTER

May Christ recognise me.
Christ relied on me.
Christ was pierced for me.
Christ on the cross for me
Christ at a loss for me.
Christ died for me.
Christ freed me.
Christ rose for me.
Christ has need of me.
Christ take pride in me.
Christ abide in me.
Christ chose me.
Christ despised for me
Christ prized by me.

AT THE EMPTY TOMB

Silence is broken, empty space redeemed.
No good looking in an empty tomb
But move on to where life teamed.
Away with long faces and gloom.
Mark recounts "Go tell the disciples" (who fail to see)
"I am going before you to Galilee."
The women fled petrified after one look.
Luke poses differently in his book
"Why seek ye the living amongst the dead?"
They told the disciples so Peter ran ahead.
Matthew tells us the Marys find
The tomb is empty and are assigned
To tell the disciples Galilee is where
They will encounter their Master dear.
John fills out the picture even more:
Mary Magdalen no gardener saw
But surprised by Jesus to her relief,
Is warned ere ascension not to cling.
What change in the Son had God begun?
Her report causes Peter and John to run
And see for themselves this challenging thing.
Bold Peter enters first. John finds belief.

HIDE & SEEK. REVELATION BY DEGREES.

Like Salome shedding her veils
While still preserving some modesty
We seek God who lingers behind
Willing us on as we will Salome
To shed the final drape. Drawing aside
Those curtains of discovery in our mind
There lurks another at the back right
Beyond which God beckons us inside
For further revelation, examining His mystery.
Veiled in flesh the Godhead see
Is but a glimpse to whet the appetite
For more. For answered Word no-one fails.
With fusion of thoughts there's no delusion
Nor with God can there be confusion.

RESURRECTION

Two men in bright white said "He has risen,
he is not here." They bade those women sad
Return to tell the disciples they would see,
Despite hesitating, Jesus in Galilee.
Many fans would think them quite mad:
The dead don't return as if arisen.
Why do you seek the living among the dead?
It all seems strange, hard to believe;
The impossible is overcome with faith,
Mystery remains not worship of a wraith.
Holy Spirit will the despondent relieve
Don't you remember what he said?
He's risen indeed is our Easter cry
How we live must be our reply.

IT'S CHRISTMAS. (A PRAYER.)

Oxen, donkeys, chickens and all;
What a menagerie round a stall!
What a cacophony of noise
Greeted the Christ child instead of toys.
Strangers, wise men, brought gifts rare,
Gold, frankincense and myrrh.
Poor shepherds hurried from their flocks
Bringing wool for a pair of socks.
Thus God clothed the Word made flesh for all to see
Giving us Holy Spirit to like him be.
Now we thank you God for family and home
Ever eager at Christmas your son will come.
But with so many parcels around our tree
Please help us make room in our hearts for Thee.

2015 CHRISTMAS THOUGHTS

Christmas comes round once again
All repeat the old refrain;
Cool Yule, Yule Rules. Stockings strain.
In a manger a babe is laid.

It's Black Friday to make you spend.
Eager sharks credit extend;
At extortionate rates they lend.
What stars the Magi send?

Syria is a pile of rubble,
No place to share a hubble-bubble.
Alliances appear crossed double.
Shepherds call crossing cold stubble.

Dictators rage feeling inferior,
They need to guard their posterior;
No safety in their lands' interior.
Joseph foils Herod's motives ulterior.

Egypt Isaiah says is a broken reed
Too much we see the country bleed.
Elsewhere escape many plead.
Yet they nurtured God's new seed.

Palestine no longer allowed pride,
Marginalised She's pushed aside,
Her own territory is denied.
May all in our Lord abide.

CHRISTMAS CHEER, PAST CHRISTMAS BLACKMAIL

God rest you merry gentlemen
This news will you dismay
The season of good will's forsaken
There's a strike on every day
For others no thoughts taken
Reconciliation's far away.
Sad tidings of disruption no joy
Strikers are out all day

It's principles, pensions not pay
No trains, no travel, no post,
Total inconvenience
Forget your turkey roast
Bring all to a total standstill
When goodwill all should boast
Sad tidings of disruption no joy
Strikes continue all day.

You unions get round table
You bosses show less greed
And with true love and brotherhood
Settle differences with speed
Embrace Christmas spirit
Give life a proper lead
Sad tidings of disruption no joy
Strikes don't win the day.

Be not friends of Satan
The Good News is to end all strife
Not holidays on hold
But to give great good cheer in life
A season to be jolly
Divisions should not be rife
Sad tidings of disruption no joy
We don't need strikes today.

We might not love our neighbor
But bloody-mindedness won't work
Bugger all, on yer bike,
Not everyone's a jerk.
To forfeit goodwill
Will lose every rewarding perk.
Sad tidings of disruption, no joy
Let Jesus lead the way.

MAGI

Wise men, we don't know how many
Sought a child, but not just any
Their astrology and calculations
Led to their perambulations.

Coming from out the East to see
Pointed to a scion of Jesse
They followed bright stars' alignment
To Mary in her confinement.

Stars as arranged their indication,
Herod's team gave validation.
Scriptures searched soon revealed
Where the promise might be sealed.

The old fox's cunning they distrusted
Since for the death of rivals he lusted;
Unaware of their complicity
They fueled tyrant insecurity

In their wake their straight sagacity
Fired his rage so implicitly
He killed in retaliation
Babies without hesitation.

Bethlehem their destination
Imagine their elation
Finding in this situation
The child of reconciliation.

They approached surroundings shambolic
Offering gifts greatly symbolic
Gold for kingship would render
Solvency where means were slender.

Frankincense with pleasing odor
Symbolized priestly prayers of candor;
Myrrh a disinfectant of old
Martyrdom to follow foretold.

So satisfied by what they found
Knowing their wisdom was that sound
The Magi went upon their way,
Joseph and Mary showed no dismay.

In turn the Holy Family left,
Herod left some mothers bereft
Of babes, refugees Egypt bound
Keeping the Christ child safe and sound.

BRANGWIN AT TAOMINA

Frank Brangwyn, R A, painted a mural,
Strictly speaking a dining room frieze,
Casa Cuseni, celebrating male love,
Restricted UK below, wild freedom above
In Sicily across those deep blue seas,
Art Nouveau style, decor all floral.
His patron Robert Hawthorn Kitchen,
Locomotive manufacturing founded,
Adopted with his partner an orphan boy,
Victim of Etna's fire, to all their joy.
Homosexual rights, society hounded,
This painted manifesto with children
Is an early story not lacking grace
Where Brangwyn's gardens surround the place.

CONTEMPLATING MONASTIC LIFE

God focused rule by Benedict
Ordered monastic routine bound
Daily prayer to life so strict
That worship painted the daily round.
"Listen with the ears of your hearts"
Is his starting point, firm advice
For those not in monastic walls found
So spirituality starts
Invading busy lives, concise
Yet rewarding rule, no burden
But a way to be. Surround
Of calm and measured pace then
Eases individuals to achieve
More than what they might believe.

ST ENODOC

                    The church where John Betjeman is buried, N Cornwall

Solid stone church engulfed by sand
Remained near buried many a year
Emerging intact with bent spire erect
After dunes were scraped away
When part exposed one day
By powerful westerly storm
That had buried it before. Wear
Well those aisles with solid stone encased
Surrounded by reclaimed land
Now grassed golf course that contours form.
In death a favourite spot select
Betjeman has this churchyard graced.
Wrecked Maria Assumpta adds fame
While St Enodoc remains a name.

BLACKFRIARS. SUNDAY AFTER WEEK OF PRAYER.

The chapel fills, greetings grow.
What hubbub. Then in float
Musicians until a tuning note
Sounds for the ensemble to flow.
Minions have placed a visible altar,
Ciborium, cloths, chasubles, candles and chalice
Wine and wafers. There's no organ, no Tallis.
White habited friars process without falter
To break bread and God's Word, make prayer.
4 pillars of commitment, study and share,
Focus on the Beatitudes
That outlines our best attitudes,
The order's compassion remind
Mission of those Dominicanly inclined.

ST BRIDES.*

Visit St Bride's on Fleet Street hill
Tiered steeple not intended by Wren
To inspire wedding cakes layered to thrill.
Within the singing uplifts the heart
And music sets the soul apart
Tired spirits with new vigor fill.
Bombs of war saw fabric broken
But sense of purpose could not kill.
Three times rebuilt, post fire restored
Saxon remains found under-floored.
Source of printed words, to the newspaper world
Well lettered spiritual home unfurled,
Here the Guild memorials hold
Life in prayer and praise enfold.

* Spiritual home of TH.

ST BRIDES SERMON.

> Reflecting on a sermon at St Brides
> by the Dean of Westminster @ 1973.

Take the waiting out of wanting. New reality,
So to his subject warmed the preacher.
The most iniquitous words in advertising
Messaging Mammon's materialism in life.
We are called to wait on God's word of silence,
Not count worth in the pounds, shillings and pence,
Striving for goods leading to greater strife.
Thus the crafted sermon started criticizing,
Comparing human values that the teacher
Set against the power of spirituality
To redeem the individual's personality.
No answer measures decisions for better quality.
God's utter silence is quieter than the height
Of Heaven's starry buzz in the stillness of the night.

LLANTONY ABBEY.*

Llanthony Priory stands alone below the border,
Shadowed by hills topped by ancient erections,
Offa's Dyke, dug long before at his directions
To keep in check restless tribes without order,
Established in a valley well watered.
Augustinian priests with their black habits
Taught there until eclipsed and daughtered
By their lesser house but more accessible
In Gloucestershire. Monks took possession,
Away from English wars of Norman succession,
Of the new church, to St John the Baptist altared,
Site of St David's ruined chapel, possible
When adopted eleven hundred by a retiring knight
To serve his heavenly Master and write.

* Vale of Ewyas, founded 1100 by Walter de Lacy.

ARMAGEDDON: BC 1457–AD 1918

Reckoned to be associated with Destiny
From historical times where Canaanite
Fought Egyptian with cataclysmic results,
Where Josiah met his end, strategic site,
God's place, Megiddo, gained identity
As final Armageddon, with notoriety
Fostered by false beliefs and assumptions;
To say nothing of depressing calculations.
God's timeline is his own. Human actions
Accumulate their consequences
Fueling fantastic prophecies, evoked
When there lingers in the collective memory
Certain facts of our ancient story
Leading to finality lacking glory.

ARMISTICE CENTENARY

Pain is linked to creation as every mother knows.
Wounded and bereaved cry more in their loss,
Tragic legacy of war, man's inhumanity to man,
When armies to their Armageddon ran.
Where is creativity in war midst destruction its gloss?
Only grief and gore with mercy in cameos.
History teaches with memories expressed
'Tis truth tyrants want suppressed.
Unremembered where born less later visits
Nor mandarin of nursery language makes sense.
Softer my experience peace keeping sits,
Though in danger from both sides, less tense
Since I support the values of where I live
To keep freedom of expression alive.

WISDOM

What is Wisdom? Is it knowing
Braking distances and slowing
When there's snow or children crossing?
Maybe after dinner giving teeth a flossing?
Perhaps she's found on the ground
Watching scatty dogs chase around
Since seeing must improve the mind
By learning about things we find.
Surely there's more to Wisdom than meets the eye?
Wisdom teeth don't represent all you know
From all you've experienced 'ere you die;
The brain isn't saturated should it slow.
The Beginning of Wisdom, not cowering in fright,
Is the fear of God living life in Christ's light.

PULL TO GOD

When darkness blankets our lives
We grow towards the light.
When we cannot tread the path alone
We begin to find support.
When our hold on life grows short
Weary prayers become a groan,
We seem lost in endless night
While God within still thrives.
We need to give Him space;
In silence do we hear his voice?
In water does the heart rejoice
Incapable of seeing his face?
God for a moment is there, hard to find,
Gone before leaving light of love behind.

BIRTH OF THE WORD

The Spirit brooded over the face of the waters.
There was movement answering speech
Even as pollen attracts bees,
As sperm to egg, Romeo to Juliet,
Creating silent sound like wind in the trees.
What we cannot see we might feel unheard
Caresses on the cheek by the breeze
When the spirit utters. The world stutters
Meaning, embryo formed, aims described,
Word at communion imbibed.
Noiselessly something said stirs, Word,
One day telling another age by age
While God calls forth creation stage by stage.

CHRISTMAS CARD

An interesting year was had by all
As soon as t'was spring it seemed to be fall
The heat of summer made us all gasp
Global warming keeps all in its grasp.
Felix gave GCSE his best shot
Getting A stars save art in the lot.
Now he's behind the wheel learning to drive
The cost of insurance will keep him alive.
Poppy all set to re-train as a nurse
At least the NHS can get no worse,
Jonah has left home to earn his own keep
Making those huts like those who tend sheep.
Briony's house a Grand Design on TV
Amazingly different as any can be.
Sorrel back in Leeds still teaching IT
Establishing the course at Trinity.
Liz gets sabbatical with books to write
On spiritual direction casting fresh light.
This verse's author expects a new eye
Sculpture's dead he gives poetry a try
All printed with linos but will anyone buy?
The reality of Christmas seems a far cry;
May it be meaningful. What more can I say?
Bold Brexit decisions care of Mrs May?
New year's surprises wait for unwrapping
With world trade sources ready for tapping.

FOURTHOUGHTS OF KELLS

What more can we learn from the Book of Kells?
What background do monk's illumination
Illustrate in fourfold gold dimensions?
Lozenge shaped truth, world's directions,
Cardinal virtues – wisdom, moderation,
Justice, fortitude – while each humor tells
Like the elements in a human story
Descriptive of any poet with his pen
Melancholic, choleric, phlegmatic, sanguine
Contrasting like the seasons. Mankind's sin
Is self; now failure, pride, lust laid open.
All is seen in the light of God's glory.
Incarnation leads to resurrection,
Eternal life the gift of salvation.

CUDDESDON

What future bishops went frantic in the attic,
Looked out on pastures green unfolding below
Before rising to the skyline, theology done,
While they contemplated future ministry?
Now they cram for ordination
Hardly aware of the breaking blossom
In the orchard nor autumn's fallen apples.
They start training like apples fully formed
Contradicting their own development
Before e'er they begin to blossom as priests:
Theological college emphasis shifts
Trying to discern those spiritual gifts.
Intense unmeasured worship lost in awe
Eclipses the gentle rhythm of yore.

VOCATION

My army friend was himself;
He served us. He served God.
He had a roguish side. He had an Olympic side.
He was our padre, but above all just Baz.
Had I traveled into a war zone?
Had I joined the army to know myself,
To push my boundaries, not just pride?
Yes. But not as I expected just to be me.
That nagging call from God I could answer
Not in the footsteps of the General
Though soldiering came easily,
But after t'other Grandfather, the priest.
That was my calling I had to answer
Even though I felt I offered the least;
Not necessarily stop wearing khaki
Nor no longer see life through sculptor's eyes,
Nor to put on a God-suit living lies.
Life is richer for experiences before
Where individuals can offer a better norm.
This was my metamorphosis to be fuller,
More complete with changed uniform
I would be seen differently, undamaged,
In a new identity Spirit managed.

WINDING STAIR TO THE PULPIT.

            Notre Dame Cathedral, Toronto.

String music fills the lower registers;
Notre Dame Cathedral's gothic grandeur
Glows blue inside. Windows depict
French settlement. Almost music hall
Capacity caters for crowds when worship
Was Sunday's occupation, far cry
From Inuit and Eskimo villages
Or chaplains besting horse copers
The price of a nag, or squally bay
Christianised Bay of Mary's Morning Sickness,
Not Seasick Bay. What message does the priest
Ascending the winding stair to the pulpit
Preach to the assembly who braved stormy trip
Anticipating freedom of true worship?

DREAMING & SLEEPING

I went to the pictures last night
I said in the morn to my Mum when small.
Dreams took me to places
Introduced strange faces
Revealed things to later befall
Putting life in a specific light.
To sleep no more a falling sense like gravity's pull
Nor a mouth never dummied that is full.
Years later such sensation
Was identified suckling my Mother's breast,
Almost asleep, satisfied, secure; realization
Of falling is the putting down to rest.
Experiencing God's love is this the best?

HUMAN BUSINESS

Human business a background roar
Tidal rush hour's steady drone,
Commuters, lorry convoys moan
Like restless waves tugging the shore.
Amongst the poplar stands with bramble walls
Birds chatter their availability
Announce for partners their eligibility.
Dog puts protective pheasant up a tree.
Hind and fawns leave off grazing
Moving to safer distance and gazing.
Roaming badger, whose numbers boom,
Displaces plovers their eggs to consume.
Raided quarry now declines; Brock's scraped
Pungent latrines mark feast from nests raped.

Out in the World

FAKE NEWS I

> Truth will out. Trumping.

I was there so it did happen:
He was not it did not therefore.
Fake news, false news, alternative facts;
How does the media treat men's acts?
Politicians make their points more.
Economical with the truth then
Used to be the situation.
Now it depends on inclination
To bolster power's position
Or how it suits the teller's mission.
Just like Guernica fact is denied
However hard perpetrators tried
To suppress facts and the truth. Reality
Exists for those with discerning ability.

FAKE NEWS II

Searching for truth that endures.
Bright light diffuses yet I see
Through pinholes greater clarity.
The Church throughout the ages has evolved
Faced with heresy some truth was solved
Keeping, not rejecting common belief.
Yet factions break away as a thief
Who only understands naturally
His own faith fundamentally.
Since Christian times Triumvirates' hours
Expire 3-2-1-None losing power.
Luther caused a stir – then Reformation.
In turn French and Russian revolutions
Toppling Tsars erased priests as their solutions.
Independent, Anglicanism maintains station.

US VALUES

Deep in the American psyche sown
Pilgrim Fathers and others buried hunger
Seeking freedoms from constraints
Alongside new opportunities to create wealth.
The new constitution made provision
For federal independence: they say
Civil War that preceded united states
Was the bloodiest known, just won;
Soldiers mown down by Gatling gun
Leaving an armed legacy, ignoring health
To shoot out individual private hates,
Assassinate their presidents.
Their Gospel of Prosperity, material reward,
Is not an outcome true Christians applaud.

BETTER VALUES

My love for Jesus remains as man to man
AGAPE rather than EROS
But to the Holy Spirit it's answering
To her call as man to woman.
As Trinity cannot be separated
Into parts dividing the unity
So love needs containing within passion
Not running carnally amok
Bridging what Greek describes
As individual characteristics
Components of the whole:
Our one word LOVE too easily
Erodes beyond the meaning meant.
In translation much more is lent.

Reflections
on Bible Passages

PSALMS 8, 144, 80, 122

What is life without purpose? Others.
What is purpose in life? Serve brothers.
What is Man that thou art mindful of him?
Let thy hand be upon the Son of Man
To show us the way that we may live
And not go back from the God we know,
Whose countenance makes us whole.
Jerusalem a symbol of unity and peace
Whose prosperity we promote
Since she is the source where Word made flesh.
You remembered him and looked after him
At whose hand there was understanding
With healing for all of mankind
Who keep Jerusalem in mind.

PATTERNS FOR PRAYER

Think of the Arran your Granny might knit
A loop of prayer, with patterns to fit
Your family name with symbols to match.
The Basket stitch for an abundant catch,
To please fishermen or fishers of men, a gem.
Cable stitch suggests an anchorage emblem
Firmly holding in God. Honeycomb stitch
Reminds us of bees' busy-ness and reward
For work done, leading to Diamond switch,
Symbol of success, treasure and wealth.
Irish Moss is a background for harvest and health.
Finally Blackberry stitch for well being to afford
A fruitful life at the very least
Leading, thornless, to the heavenly feast.

A WORD IN TIME

The Word was reason to distinguish
Good from evil, and had hung on the tree
To enlighten those who ate, let them see
With opened eyes to choose and discern God's wish
For honest appreciation, company
Best understood as adoration.
The Word as flesh is impeccable, unblemished,
Personable, persuasive, undiminished,
Enabling trust to sift advantageous from harm
Using our freewill Godwards, without alarm,
Weighing the odds in considered moderation
As conscience, soul, and rationality
Dictate within individual experience:
Sure fruit expressing truth and sense.

JOHN 1, V5.

> The light shines in the darkness,
> and the darkness comprehended it not.

The Darkness comprehendeth not the Light.
Light understands dark whereby we see and know
Recognizing truth and naming creation
As Adam at the beginning station
When God formed other life and creatures low
Having separated day from night.
This light was embraced by the Word as life
Revealing truth, grace, and God's love for all.
The Word became flesh through Incarnation
Matched at mortal end by resurrection.
Those disciples who answered Jesus' call
Preached his Word as peace amongst worldly strife
That those accepting him him become, then led,
Spared all judgment, at communion fed.

LAZARUS, THE DISCIPLE WHOM JESUS LOVED.*

They told Jesus 'He whom you love is ill,'
But he delayed three days and found him dead.
Deeply moved 'See how he loved him,' they said.
Commanded 'Lazarus come forth' the tomb he left.
Reclining close at dinner he asked who will
Betray Jesus who passed the sop. Bereft
At the foot of the cross bidden alone
To care for Jesus' mother as his own.
Faster than Peter he saw and believed;
Seeing folded grave clothes all doubts relieved.
He recognized Jesus on the shore
When their fishing nets could hold no more.
Curious, once dead would he die again?
Answer: 'Until I come he's to remain.'

---

* John 11 v3,36; 13 v23; 19 v26; 20 v2; 21, v7,20.

TO THE CHILDREN OF THIS AGE.*

Hear ye peoples about the Lord.
You have mouths but neither worship
Nor speak of the Lord your God.
You have ears but hear not his Word.
You have noses but scent not truth.
You have eyes but disregard God.
You have feet but walk not in his Way.
You have hands but hold no body
Nor a nourishing sacrament. Good for nowt,
You are like the idols of old, pure chance,
Yet worshiped for indulgence. Lordship's out
Alien to you save for arrogance.
Alas you children of this age
There is God but you don't engage.

---

* Psalms 115, vv3-8; 135, vv15-18: Jeremiah 10, vv1-10.

SALOME'S DANCE*

                                    Matthew 14; Mark 6.

Salome danced, shedding seven veils,
Nubility revealed, nobility's eyes peeled.
Ability to arouse never fails,
Fanfare as Herod vain promises sealed.
Orange for dreams a few might share;
Red for passion running strong in the veins;
Yellow for reason to blind the glare;
Green for bliss all hope life gains;
Purple for compassion and lending aid;
Blue for knowledge not to be gain-said;
White for courage. Thus symbols shed
Leaving a dangerous path to tread.
Morals to the very winds cast aside
Left John beheaded, his truth denied.

* Attributed to Herodias' Daughter as Dance of the Seven Veils.

A THOUGHT FOR CHRISTMAS

Released from lockdown we can entertain
Thoughts of returning to normality
Hoping for a Christmas of quality
With Felix from Edinburgh by train.
We hope to see Poppy and co not in vain
And glimpses of Briony and Sorrel gain.
Liz on Zoom, it weren't much fun
But courses continue once begun.
What's seen church crawling I turn to print
Not just a view through a leper's squint.
Fieldfares and Redwings augur cold days,
Sloe Gin, Christmas fare and displays.
We wish you the best, take every care,
And churches open for carols and prayer.

WHO IS GOD?

Emotional attributes replace carnal
Lusts of old, abstract reality,
Now seen embodied in creation
Where human form is an aspect
Bound by a Spirit of creativity.
Merciful, forgiving, a God of promise
Whose Word calls forth Life in community
Although couched in enduring silence.
His wavelength communicates
A way of life easier lived
Without burden or restriction,
But peace of mind to weed out darnal
Choking the yield of a fruitful life
Replacing with healing, curtailing strife.

CITY WALLS ABOUND

Old walls surround, enclosing, embracing,
Shielding all within outward facing,
Decaying, eroding with age and rain,
Withstanding siege and war, yet strain
Against collapse foundations undermined
When seeping water their weak points find.
Local stone hewn and cut, sorted and laid
Interlocking with gatehouses splayed.
Hezekiah's tunnel the well accessed
Outside Jerusalem's walls when pressed.
Omri had Samaria's stones shaped like wedges
Packed tighter when foes battered the outer edges.
York's ancient defenses comprise Roman courses
Below medieval stones to defy Lancastrian forces.

A WEDDING POEM*

Life comes round full circle, rotate,
Epitomized by the arrival of Spring
As Creation resurrects to a new cycle, spate
Of courtship described, no mere fling
As the turtle dove calls for a mate:
Amongst the flowers it is time to sing.
So the husband is urged to value and receive
His wife that each to the other may cling
Completing the cleaving of Adam to Eve
As one once more – a mysterious thing.
Thus from marriage we learn truth's ring
That Christ like the groom takes under his wing
His bride, us the church. That sense of care
Is for us all, in an everyday sense, to share.

---

* Song of Solomon 2 v10–15; Ephesians 5, v25–end.

VALUING

What is an encounter without value?
Everyone is worth God's love
So why not all others with whom we share
A passing moment, spell of sustained care,
One way or another respect is due,
Indebtedness to our Lord and Gov?
For that person, whether stranger or friend
More than one good turn deserves another
Regardless that they're not sister nor brother.
Recognizing their worth is to ascend
Finding increase in one's estimation
Not disappointment but germination.
They are like sparkles in a shower when raindrops glint
Sun-struck amongst leaves, of fine weather a hint . . .

THE COMFORTER

Whence comes the Comforter? Personified
From Isaiah's utterance of future hope
Her presence is promised post- resurrection,
From the beginning master workman's inspiration,
Pre-eminent, unconfined spanning time, scope
For brightening life, and for those who sighed
That vacuum filled. Sent not to condemn
But strengthen the down-hearted, reprove falsehood,
Contradicting lies, revealing truth to the receptive,
The Counselor called to be alongside to revive
All who flag, releasing Wisdom, encouraging the good.
Ever present her delight is in the sons of men;
Restoration is foretold, iniquities folded away,
Like wind across wheat holding all in her sway.

CATHOLIC & PROTESTANT PERCEPTIONS

Why burden adherents with rules to follow
When faith is there to liberate the spirit?
Worship comes through service to others
Rather than putting self first. As mothers
Expect fair play within a family knit
By Christian values why let faith leave hollow
Community life with false regulations
When Christ labored to remove restrictions
To allow all to respond in spirit and in truth?
Us Protestants are by no means uncouth
But enjoy a freedom to Catholics denied
Yet our needs are by the Spirit supplied.
Dictats from celibates in ivory towers
Cannot immunize the Holy Trinity's powers.

THE NEW ISRAEL*

Do I detect a change of personality?
Do you express yourself with new reality?
Once you yearned for a land of milk and honey
With freedom of religion, your own money,
Space in your established faith to come of age
As Bar-Mitzvah, Sons of the Commandment.
Grapes and figs symbolized this land of plenty
But with your return comes a new identity
Balfour applied with your own amendment.
As Sabras protect you with inner rage
Strident nationalism describes this prickly pear
Restricting Palestinians from what you hold dear.
Will Srulik and Handala** live side by side
Revering a promised land with equal pride?

  * Tzabar, Opuntia Cactus.
 ** Israeli & Palestinian cartoon characters.

2 TREES

Innocence fled when Eve picked fruit; what did she see?
Was it her own naked vulnerability,
Desire for Adam, or plain curiosity?
Like Pandora's Box life somehow changed:
Clothes for nakedness were exchanged,
Needs to meet own livelihood arranged.
Earthbound, paradise lost, freedom forfeit,
Left no wiser nor knowledge somehow lit
Over good and evil, life and death. Spirit
Does not lead us to despise one come to save,
Offering new life, on another tree able to brave
Scarring treatment and quit the funeral cave.
Marring him our rejection exists as unbelief
In his redeeming experience to bring relief.

THE COLT, THE FOAL OF AN ASS, IMPORTANT ON PALM SUNDAY

The excitement the occasion brought
Must have banished all thought
That I was carrying a heavy load.
Never ridden, not dismayed, no need of goad
I was chosen rather than my mother
Who had borne me, greatly burdening,
Internalized till I became other.
Previously, only a life of ease,
I had never carried anything
But today I was called to please.
Led across the valley citywards to psalms,
The going was soft, all coats and palms.
People loudly expressed their hopes realized
By the man I carried so highly prized.

FLIP SIDES OF NATIVITY AND CRUCIFIXION

Gone full term contractions start
Once the waters break, membranes part.
Practiced breathing rhythms help to push
New life into the world to breathe and cry,
Opposite the struggle for breath
Nailed on a cross to stifle and die,
Arms stretched taught, strangling,
Feet pegged so no legs dangling.
Either way the body heaves
As new born babe or as life leaves.
Who mops the brow that cloth retains
An image imprinted with the stains
Of life-bringing effort? Is crown of thorn
As triumphant as babe's crowning while born?

THE GOOD SHEPHERD*

His sheep know his old coat, recognise
Familiar noise of paper sack
Rattling contents of nuts of some kind.
Calls heard none inclined to lag behind
Following their shepherd pack on back,
Just mouthfuls each judging by its size.
Animal husbandry at best
Often takes the simplest form
Nurturing beasts without fear,
Ensuring food is always near,
Shelter from any passing storm,
Safety when laid down to digest.
By such means the priest takes stock
Entrusted by God to care for his flock.

The Good Shepherd, bronze.

* John 10; Psalm 23.

TRANSFIGURATION

Raised above daily business below
Mountain top panoramas show
A world to command as Satan
Had suggested in the wilderness.
Now Jesus with his chosen three
Seeks a seal on his ministry
With them present there to witness
What Moses and Elijah began.
Shining whiter than the best on earth
Three stood transfigured to discuss
A particular exodus
Adding to the Word greater worth
Prefiguring glory when heaven
Descended on mankind with new leaven.

EVE

An anorexic Eve could be described
The spare rib of life rather than the wife
Of Adam raised from the dust by God,
Appeared his companion from the same pod
Since both reflect his image. What strife
Followed the loss of Eden they'd imbibed.
Central to our human poem these two,
Serpent seduced, ate the fruit of knowledge
Meddling with the ripened apple or medlar
Swallowing the story that lying pedlar
Told. Between them and God this wedge
Became their bond when nakedness they knew.
Thus Eve attracted Adam's attention
But from Eden gained suspension.

CLIMATE CHANGE AND WORSE

We pollute and over-populate, burst
The planet so nature takes revenge.
Leviathan no longer plays choking
In the seas, while horsemen vent their fury;
Locusts by the swarm cross continents,
Plagues and thirst, war, Middle East's worst.
We must share and re-kindle our morality
Mankind must mend their ways, find respect
For our earthly paradise, and terminate
Rape of precious resources at others' cost
Meaning less than excavated minerals is lost.
Used products and waste contaminate
This world, which we need to value and use
Capable of meeting our needs with no abuse.

ASH WEDNESDAY 2021.

This year Ash Wednesday's a distant thought
No chance of deeper reflection
Nor usual sincere confession
After the annual incineration
Of previous Palm Crosses
To mark the forehead when penance's sought.
With social distancing touching's out;
Yet sacraments are physical demanding
Earthly human re-assurance
Not restrictions of a correct stance
Denying the agency of handling
Allowing spiritual transmission all doubt
To dispel, replace guilt with peace
That thanks to God may never cease.

DECEPTION

Deception features in Revelation
Where those who support you today
Will turn when it's ripe to have their way.
Who's the white horse rider, his commission?
Does God call up these woes to make us turn,
Repent, worship and acknowledge him?
There is no doubt if we fail to learn
And look beyond ourselves chaos reigns.
There is no peace until we love neighbors.
 Where there is danger salvation grows.
Yet we have Freewill which God allows
Who ultimately good and evil ordains.
As Jacob deceived Esau we're inclined
To obscure all God intended and designed.

PEOPLE

God created man in his own image, male and female,
Enabling each to be an equal person
To be in turn alive to each other.
Inter-relationships make for an intercourse,
Deep dialogue, recognizing the spirit in the individual.
The sculptor reads the spirit in the figure,
Contrasting birth in the spirit through water
At baptism, putting life into the sculpture
As bread puts the life of Christ in our bodies.
Behold the power and life, fire and spirit
In birth and baptism at the beginning,
Re-birth sustained through communion
Like life is cast into likeness in art.
So people are destined to be people from the start.

CREATION

God chuckled when light overcame the dark:
It had all happened from the merest spark.
He laughed to see so much water swamp the firmament,
So much so he roared and waterfalls cascaded down
Leaving dry land proud. A playful challenge, He guffawed
As He set orbs in circulation, scattering stars abroad.
Giggles ceased. It was man from dust that made him frown;
Was it really his image? Man and woman's advent;
Were both their attributes His?! Would they fare well?
What if those parameters He set they ignored?
As evening companions would they be bored?
Creation would suffer, Eden choke. Time would tell.
God smiled, if they poached the tree of knowledge
It would fruit their salvation was His pledge.

THE CUP OF BLESSING. WRATH'S CONVERSION.*

God's cup of wrath had an accumulation
A reflection of His pent up frustration
With creation deserving its presentation
To drain it without interception
As their judgment and damnation.
What Son of Adam or Daughter of Eve
Could by drinking salvation achieve
Causing the cup's curse's cancellation?
The Son of Man accepted the dedication
Giving thanks with the cup's consecration
To offer all accepting eternal preservation.
Yet in Gethsemane a moment of hesitation:
'Let this cup pass, nay thy will be done'.
Thus light shone, the Kingdom was won.

---

* Psalm 75, v8; Matt. 26, vv36–46; ditto in Mark and Luke.

ST. DAVID*

Not as ancient as Menevia by which
His abbey took its name where the switch
That saintly David bade
To a rigorous ascetic was made.
We can only guess at any source
Describing his virtues to which we cling.
Leeks strong in flavor sustain
While golden daffodils remain
A splash of colour to herald spring.
March begins with full balanced force;
Wind, gentle as a lamb or strong as a lion.
Thus a man of discipline, true Welsh scion,
And balanced strength held Brefi Synod
In five sixty outlining paths to be trod.

* d. 601.

RUTH

Boaz exercised his right as kin,
Showed Ruth favor, not forsaken,
When Moabite migrant she returned
With her mother-in-law. To be spurned
And destitute was a risk she had taken
Unless her gentle demeanor win
What was her widow's due.
Naomi, Amara, to support; bitter
Times, gleaning, to live through.
Her good fortune matched the glitter
In the landlord's eye and to satiate
When he uncovered her to consummate
Her rightful place at his side and provide
Heirs to raise a David when she died.

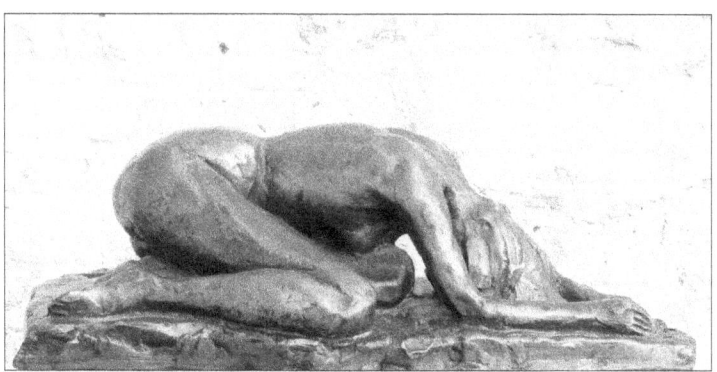

Ruth, or Humility. Bronze.

BATHSHEBA

Grass widow with husband at war
She bathed in sunshine on the upper floor.
Flash of flesh caught David's eye, lure
Exciting enough to further explore.
Thus Bathsheba, bared with sinuous limb
With a bridal figure young and slim
Was commanded to be brought to him;
Obedient subject to answer a whim.
Their union sowed unwitting seeds;
Guilt, doomed pregnancy and leads
To Uriah's death and other deeds,
Yet in time furthered Judah's needs.
Her intuition tempered warrior might
Gaining Solomon wisdom for his birthright.

ST. JH NEWMAN

What wisdom earned him sainthood?
Yet he seemed charismatic, profound,
For even no relic could be found,
Compost had rotted all away for good.
As a Tractarian, sensible.
As an evangelical, catholic.
As a catholic, evangelical.
In teaching, practical.
Conspiratio, true to form.
Conspiracy of pastors and faithful
Agree to maintain a norm.
Such heartfelt expression would pull,
Cor ad cor loquitur, far from odd
But as close as any speak to God.

Roundel for St. John Henry Newman, plaster for bronze.

BLIND BARTIMAEUS

When Blind Bartimaeus called out
All eyes turned on him. Was his chance denied?
'Don't trouble him', 'Hold your tongue,' they cried.
Remarks that made him louder shout.
He sensed his call for help was heard.
After being led over as requested
And asked what it was he wanted
To regain his sight seemed not absurd.
He didn't want his eyes to be tested
And his request was soon granted;
No spit; no parental blame; no game;
No men seen walking like trees; no shame.
With this symbolic act Jesus let men see
That his ministry was reality.

Blind Bartimaeus. Bronze.

ST. PATRICK

Taken from Bannavem when sixteen
From homely coasts Patrick as a slave
Shepherds for six years in Ireland green,
Returning when about fifty to save
And convert those he had known
In obedience to a vision when shown
Another calling in life. Apostle from 431
He focused on Leinster and Tara and won,
Much opposed by the druids of the land.
Founded Armagh cathedral when bishop,
He withdrew to Croagh Patrick's top
To fast and pray. Perhaps his hand
Collectio Canonum Hiberniae wrote
Despite little evidence of note.

GRIEF; HIS ON THURSDAY, HERS ON FRIDAY

'Let this cup pass, nay thy will be done.'
What agonies of grief, hesitation, doubt
Assailed our Lord in Gethsemane about
His Father's business. Obedience won,
Fulfilling prophecy despite the cost
That those he gathered should not be lost.
So Jesus prayed the night before
Knowing there was more agony in store.
When Friday saw him nailed to a cross
Mary could only bewail her loss.
Her grief so deep as piercing sword
To see the man that she adored,
Further fulfilling the fears of another
Knowing the grief of a Mother.

THE CALL OF THE DISCIPLES. JAMES.

The dilemma of food for all versus space.
The soil was tilled at a gentle pace
By James and his ilk using hoes,
Basic hand tools and sturdy arms.
Now soil degradation alarms:
What chemicals the farmer sows
Environmentalists trace,
How heavy machinery compacts,
How land can be better rested,
How tillage can be less invasive,
How natural nutrients survive,
How a greater norm is invested.
Land in hand for food contracts,
More mouths to feed encroach fields
Which in turn must produce increased yields.

ST. THOMAS MISSES OUT

Thomas shoulders his hod, delivery man,
Laden with goods that all demand,
Heaving parcels like an Amazon van.
Too busy to meet the rest of the band
In the upper room to share good news,
He misses the visit, demands he views
Those scars of crucifixion needing
Evidence to be convinced
The impossible happened as foretold.
Might he actually the Teacher behold
At whose death they all winced?
A heavy load of events leading
To those finding it is no wraith
That is the mystery of faith.

ST. JUDE

Even Thomas Hardy found Jude obscure
When all is based on a name in passing
Conflicting with another version;
Thaddeus doesn't ease the confusion.
Both reveal no vision encompassing
A fact or characteristic to ensure
We visualize more than his presence
As one of the twelve. Perhaps his image
Represents ourselves who follow?
We are there, faith makes each a fellow.
I portray him myself as I engage
To answer my vocation's essence.
Self-portrait in progress as I leave
To serve whom I turn to believe.

ST. MATTHEW

Counting out the money, exchange rates
Variable to maximize church tax,
Matthew sat at the receipt of custom.
Pecuniary purity from
Denarius to shekel wasn't lax
For those entering the temple's gates.
What did Jesus see in him to call?
Obedience to custom, honest
In dealing, willing to please not cheat?
Lend his name to a Gospel meet
For the Jews, fulfilling the rest
Of OT recorded prophecies all?
He paved the way as teller
And more than salvation's seller.

ST.S PETER AND ANDREW.

John pointed Jesus to Andrew, and another,
Who followed to where he was staying
And spent the day exploring praying.
Observant, he found his brother
To share revelations so fabulous.
Peter, quick to react, impetuous,
Left his nets to be a spiritual landmark
Though to begin with his faith was stark:
 The shoal of fish – incredulous:
A suffering Messiah – scandalous:
His pre-conceptions – idolatrous?
Guilty of denial – disastrous.
He became a Samson for the church
As Andrew enabled folk in their search.

THE NATIVITY.

When the waters broke no-one was there
The main room of the house was occupied. Here
We had that human space where, a bit rough,
The beasts laid or fed from a trough.
No mid-wife nor birthing stool
So I knelt and spread my thighs:
Thus Mary perched to deliver her baby;
I put pressure downwards on her shoulders
To help her push each contraction.
Being young she gave birth easily,
All happening with hardly a cry.
She held the child to her breast,
Too soon to feed until lactation,
But with joy and satisfaction,
So she wrapped him tightly
In her cloak while I strawed
A manger as a warming bed.
The beasts endorsed with their presence
Our basic nature raised by faithful sense.
Tired, she fell asleep with a smile,
Her head tilted against my side, while
I sat watching the bright moonlight outside
But an inner radiance came from the child.

CREATION

CREATION.

Nature has strong resilience,
Having on man no reliance;
Nor does she keep eery silence.
Despite species' heavy loss
At man's hands she'll survive
Long after man succumbs;
Mankind are like mere crumbs
Rubbed from bread with yeast alive.
The noise of raw nature, cross
From over exploitation,
Roars, and rends season's rotation;
Flora and fauna's expostulation
Is loss of bleat in creation,
In humans loss of sensation.

PRAYER AND THE ENVIRONMENT.

Air's turbulence becomes more extreme
Like heat agitating water in a pan.
The force of convection increases flow
Destruction's span no longer slow.
Is this chaos the fault of man
Or a natural cycle driving the scene?
Prayers to benefit creation
Need thanks to temper action,
To live useful intervention,
Doing what God might mention.
Our world is a living organism
With checks and balances in unison,
Whose needs with sensitivity
Are matched by our activity.

EVOLUTION. FALL OF A SPARROW.

If God had not intended evolution
All wouldn't be voyages of discovery but solved
Instead life of all kinds has evolved.
There is no Bible contradiction:
A day in God's time is but an age
That stretches Genesis without denying
And on spiritual wisdom relying.
Ages in geological formation beg belief
Force us in a bigger picture to engage.
Understanding God develops without restriction
Faith finalized is not a given prescription
But reliance on our own growth is relief
In itself reflecting our inner evolution
And for those who trust the perfect solution.

HARES

1.

As I climbed to stalk Glenshee
Some forty hares proceeded me;
The higher I the whiter they
Not boxing that cold October day.
At summit top the thinning grass
Meant little forage with all so sparse.
Yet sika came to higher ground
While lower down the red was found.
Below left in scree there swaggered
A stag dominance rehearsed
Undisturbed by hares dispersed
When shot glanced shoulder he staggered.
Soon on another beat Urquhart's shot
Bagged a handsome beast for the pot.

Trinity of Hares. Drawing for print. TH.

2.

Three hares in the meadow grazed
Split lipped trio heads hardly raised.
They run in circles when alarmed
Relying on their faster speed
While 3-60 vision helps escapes
Though ahead they may not notice
Someone standing still. Police
Poorly protect from coursing dogs harmed
At night for gypsy bets slipped from lead . . .
These springtime boxers fascinate,
Moon, fertility associate,
Nurture scattered young in open scrapes.
Three hares, three ears, each a pair
This Trinitarian symbol share.

Hares Boxing. Drawing for print.

SPARROW HAWK

A flurry of feathers at my feet
Upon my opening our front door;
Male sparrowhawk in taloned claw
Clutched a collared dove to eat.
Surprised he released his hold
Allowing his prey reprieve
In bramble thicket and raptor leave
Unable to follow wings fold
Despite speed, on branch alighted
To wait until frightened away,
Leaving ruffled dove delighted
To live another day,
When I approached our hens with scoop
Interrupting his murderous stoop.

CURLEW

The liquid ripple of the Curlew
Floats across the moorland heather,
Come the return as if on cue
Of sun and mild springlike weather,
Like a child's water whistle softly blown.
Crying, circling on the wind, flown
From further shores and now alone
Until its mate with wavering tone
Replies to haunt the graying dawn.
Surrounding countryside seems forlorn
Until answer proves they're safely paired.
With downward curved beak this flecked bird,
Remaining on the list of game,
Cries its bubbling phonetic name.

OWL

1.

Whence the wisdom of the Owl?
Do its looks elevate this fowl?
Sensory ears locate its prey
Difficult enough by light of day
Yet in the dusk cover's slight
Where rodents feel secure
Unaware sharp eyed silent flight
Stalks overhead to strike with claw.
Athena's attribute, symbol not minion,
Was Merlin's messenger and companion
Thus deemed wise by association:
Myth endorses such affiliation:
Strigiformes boasts some Strigidae
And one native Tytonidae.

Stylized Owl drawing.

2.

Eerily the owl quarters the ground
On silent wing across the marsh
When it's dusk with weather harsh
Seeking prey by searching sound
In feathered cups that eyes surround
Filtering faintest noises we can't hear,
But its quest no cause for fear.
Post strike the tawny is post bound
Preyed vole clutched in taloned toes.
Fur ball at tree base marks a roost
From which wavering whoos may boost
Answering hoo-hoos where another goes.
No wonder owls wisdom symbolize
Seeing in all light with saucer eyes.

Owl in Flight. Linocut print. TH.

WOODPECKER, OR YAFFLE.

Persistent chirrup long liquid chirr
Wakes me early. Woodpecker as I stir
With staccato bursts fills the air,
From some nearby tree his call he drills.
Other song too the morning air fills.
Magpie squabs squabble leaving their lair,
While the cuckoo moves further afield.
Blackbird, beak full of worms, too busy
Feeding young to sing. Stray bumble bee
Meandering now it's warmer soars on.
Monotonous as the day draws on
Constant roocoos plainly pigeon peeled
Dominate dawn like village church bells.
From sweet pollinators no incessant buzz swells.

GEESE.

Gossiping geese gargle, a gaggle,
Which honked their skein through the air,
Folding their wings tails a-waggle
Standing tall on the edge of a mere,
Having regained their composure
After sliding on the ice landing,
Arriving with others footing unsure
Crashing their group before banding
To graze the grass on water's edge
Poking for grubs amongst the sedge.
Symbol of gathered Holy Spirit
Those behind in wedge-shaped flight
Honk to encourage their leader's pace
Until they change order without disgrace.

DANDELION

Dandelions in the nearby paddock yield
To buttercups their graying locks
Beloved of children as parachute clocks.
Dotted yellow in summer months this field,
Bounded by stands of willow and poplar,
Shows natural arcs of seed-falls fanned
In scattered carpets to take their stand;
One grazes like attic cobwebs the surface
'Mongst grass green and lush having been grazed
By sheep soon shorn their lambs now raised.
Children under chins t'other place
Reflecting a penchant for butter so popular.
St George's Day was hardly fine
Now too late for dandelion wine.
Satellites now farmers tell
Where to plant so crops grow well.

HAZE OF SLOES.

Froth of Blackthorn blossom become blue-hued
Berries blurred with a bloom rendering these sloes
Purple, wreathed in a backdrop of green
Or dying yellow leaves slowly falling. Keen
Frost browns them until stripped when wind blows
Away cover to bare twigs fruit-sprued.
Drops of rain might remain with crystal glint
While there is sunshine at sufficient angle
Post the autumn equinox to bathe the tops
Along the path in brighter light. Such plentiful crops
Harbinger harsh winter. The wayside tangle
With pre-amble of autumnal tint
Will flatten with frost and snow
Whilst our sloe gin will keep hearts aglow.

MORE DOG WALKING.

I built a dam today
Stream's flow blocked with rocks across
Causing bubbles by the flow's loss
To change their psalmody.
Different pitch of melody
Burbling from the blockage
Stemming flooding rage.
Water levels rising
Cause detours round the edge,
Unsure stepping stone a wedge
Where sundry debris cling
Of bigger scale a parody.
Never mind the watery spread
The dog catlike leaps ahead.

ODE TO DOGS

Most dogs prove a loyal friend
Who make demands for a walk,
Some by your leave are wont to retrieve
Returning with objects you send,
Or head cocked listen while you talk
With steady gaze lapping up praise
Tail wagging, no squirrels to stalk.
Some like most to pee every post,
Desire a good bed, to be well fed
To lie in the sun and roast.
Dogs pull a face when in disgrace,
Ears flat, they soon learn your ways;
Some after training from puppyhood refraining
Do as you ask whatever the task.

DOG WALK DOWN THE LANE. WALKING IN THE WOOD.

Walking in the whispering woods
Leaves above rattled in wind's murmur
Those below rustled underfoot.
Laughing Yaffle, undulating moods
Like its flight, marked its departure.
Incubated pheasant poults piped, grown
Lamp brooded their mothers unknown,
Somewhat lost till put to flight.
Bird-foil scent dog distracting lies,
Badger bramble berry gorged absurd
Had made a scrape to dump his turd
Out of proportion to his size
But not his appetite. From game crops in alarm
Rose small murmurations of finch by the charm.

GARDEN OUTSIDE THE WINDOW.

The dead leaves rustled
As blue tits bustled
Flipping them over for grains
Under rose and hellebore
Or scurried left to right
Along the window ledge
Hopeful of some insect store
Or putty moist in window panes.
Perky wren hopped t'other way
Should some tit-bit be astray
Whilst sparrows worked the hedge
As any host or quarrel might.
Jay scolded the woods, no goldfinch bellow,
Nor in conventicle magpies like methodists mellow.

DAWN BREAKS THROUGH THE BEDROOM WINDOW OR THE CUCKOO.

The cuckoo cucked no answering coo
The owl t-witted no echoing t-woo.
Where are the birds we like to hear?
Their food is stolen – the bloody cat I fear.
Less little birds in hedgerows trill
Blooming' pheasants eat their fill
The farmer leaves no headland
The bloody cat stalks near at hand . . .
The bloody cat kills birds all day.
The bloody cat destroys owls' prey
Set the dogs on bloody cats
Impossible to confine to killing rats,
Chain them to domestic mats.
Confine them all to blocks of flats.

STORM OPHELIA.

In the shadow of Storm Ophelia.

Mid-day sun blood red espied
As if still dawn lingered
Hurricane's false distortions ply
Refracting light strangely red
Mingled with Saharan dust.
Wind's strengthening gust
Buffets those outside.
It feels a storm is brewing
Scented atmosphere stewing
With light so discolored.
But that onslaught's to the West
Giving Celtic clans little rest
From the turmoil near the eye
As close isobars pass them by.

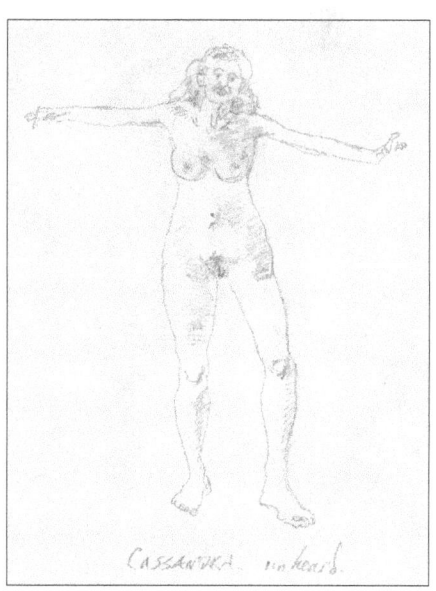

Drawing for Stations of the Odyssey, ignored Cassandra rends her garments.

30/11/17

Night frost has crisped and clamped nature
Leaving landscape with an opaque sheen
As artist might cover canvas to cure
With a wash like haze of polish before
Antique table top is all dry then buffed.
So the sun brightens the colors
Reducing covering on grass ice fluffed
To glistening globules yet in the shadows
Is no competitor against the cold
Nor in hollows which rime did enfold
Save under mature trees that retain
Warmth as armpits might for numb hands.
Ground bound dog startles then tracks leaping
Squirrel through higher branches' safekeeping.

PLOUGHING WITH HORSES.

Harnessed heavy horses bend necks to pull the plough,
Calling them on, my hands steadying the blade
Shearing and turning soil leaving enough
Furrow so one horse in lower trench bade,
T'other walked the length on higher firm ground.
This experience of a bygone age
Resurrected some familiar truths round
The ploughman who had companionship
With uncomplaining team, friendship,
Periods of rest, no engine straining rage,
While the tractor driver of today
Is a lone soul with radio on play
With many horse power against my two
Whose only falter may be loss of shoe.

STOLEN MOMENTS

Bother those who switch the clocks
Mucking about with time of day.
When dark the extra hour to woo
Is forfeit when sun means more to do.
Now while I might linger and stay
In spring shortened summer day mocks
Our hurried intimate moment.
Average is no compensation
For such untimely interruption
When what lighter day cannot lend
Gladly's stolen at year's back-end.
Time for a lingering kiss is well spent.
Encouraged to enjoy an embrace
Any denial is a disgrace.

Hillside Parish Magazine Cover.

TO THE BELOVED

Pleasing perfume pervades the air,
Softening senses sweet subtle scent
From the Rambling Rector's dome
Cascading with flowers frothing foam
Cover summer house with blossom bent
Extending aroma by petals scattered
Around the Beloved's bower in trails.
Crown of clouds above stream mares' tails
Like smoke from birthday cake candles blown
Signifying wind and rain will leave tattered
This temporary fragrance delights strewn.
Tended to brighten up our home,
Effort and attendance rendered not in vain
To nurture such a flourish to kisses gain.

ANOTHER ROSE

Single roses blossom fragrant full
Paler colors mean stronger scent
Save deep damson red with a twist
Of petals giving aroma like mist
So olfactory glands are pent
Enjoying what no flower can dull.
Is Florry Bunder a gardener wonder?
Might she cleave these buds asunder?
When opened out there's released heady
Perfume conjuring closeness desire
Linking intimacy remembered ready
Kindling anew that inner fire.
Unseen the Beloved hovers close
Intoxicating as any rose.

FAMILY YEAR

To review a year is no simple task.
What to put in, who did we ask?
Here and abroad comings and goings
In the garden what of our sowings?
Sculpture proves a non-earner
Liz writes formation for the learner.
Felix proves quite a discerner
On various doings at school:
Karate, skateboard, farming all cool.
Whilst he has been occupied
Liz and I Sicily espied.
Circuiting Northern Ireland, Donegal;
To Celtic Meath we made a passing call
Coasts, Causeway to cloisters and crosses tall.

Felix, 3, with his pedal car.

PATIENCE.

> Placed providentially. A Holiday Game.

Patience can be hard:
It hinges on an opportune card,
Turned up by lucky coincidence;
To keep, when moved to fill the space,
Sequences growing, the suits in place.
Does this illustrate God's providence
When things come together, make sense?
The input is our own with what comes our way
So God may place a person where one day
They best meet another's stated need,
With prayer some situation feed
Or sow some spiritual seed.
Timely met, quiet, better prepared,
Listening sees such a speaker spared.

CORNWALL SURFERS. HOLIDAY TIME.

Presage of storm sharp edged slate blue sky*
Wind whipped sand clears beaches, screens fly
Driving folk back to holiday lets.
Empty car parks, dead bbqs, nets
Not set, chippies expect a mob.
Wrapped warm in wet suits surfers bob,
Ride dying waves; another day
Wild rollers from deep sea their skills
Will outperform so tumbling spills
Will be their lot in welters of spray.
All anticipate the weather
Consult their app to plan whether
Favored sport is on or should they
Visit English Heritage next day.

* Penumbra of torrent that washed out Coverack 18/7/17.

DAYMER BAY

Microcosms of Cornwall's slighting
Sand castles await destruction
By the incoming evening tide biting
When waves below the moat explode
Bastion battlemented walls erode.
Soon sands show smoothed overnight
No sign of pediment nor pier laid
Nor even foundations remain
Come morning when again
Architects and builders construction
Make with bucket and spade
Unless delayed or driven by rain.
This endless summer cycle continues
Through the generations to amuse.

2018 HOGMANAY HANGOVER

Early escaping extended entertainment
Artificially hollow to mark time's space
Till firework finale greets attainment
On beginning New Year at holiday pace.
Empty exuberance precedes abandoned
Resolutions freshly made round fond
Themes molded in life's rat-race
To seize abstract opportunities, certainment,
But never really openly on offer.
Familiarity instrumental for Hogmanay
Consumes hospitality others proffer
Before all go on their alcoholic way.
'Gainst this backdrop of familiarity and fraud
All and sundry embark again to seek life's reward.

INDIGNITIES

Granny would grab my arms to twist
As if I were double jointed
When I was small, hands pointed
To put on my coat or make a fist
To plunge down sleeves seemingly squashed
With woollie too big beneath new washed.
Thus trussed totally 'gainst winter chill
In green tweed with pixie hood, same old drill.
This routine struggle left hunched
Memories of restrictions,
Reduced movement, collar bunched
Despite doting intentions.
Now loving spouse holds my coat wide
So my hands into armholes can slide.

MODELS & MINIATURES

All my own was my boyhood world
I controlled my trains and laid track
To make a place in my mind's eye
All around the floor. Boxes became my
Imaginary industrial units, unfurled,
Served by slab-sided tank engines all black
Shunting jostling goods wagons past
Long before our container age excess.
The outer circuit without fail
Occupied the green flying express
With liveried carriages like a tail,
Maroon and cream, Royal Mail last
Carriage collecting postbags in its rear.
It was only whistles I did not hear.

LEEDS SCULPTURES

Morn and Even stand alternate around
Leeds City Square holding their torches unlighted
Aloft with their drapery loose blown
Revealing their soft curves and firm round
Breasts but their bronze buttocks blighted
By the pitting of acid rain where no gown
Adds thickness to the metal need filling
Or by artisan's hand tapping and drilling.
Round its centerpiece of horsed Black Prince,
Potent symbol of pride these ladies eight
By Alfred Drury celebrate light,
And wealth of city fathers evince.
Bare statement of civic success Circe stands
Magic wand and empty chalice in her hands.

NOVEMBER.

*"November is such disagreeable month, said Meg. That's
why I was born in it" said Jo, her sister." Little Women.*

There is little to commend November:
Autumn colour has faded
Cold and mist have invaded
Summer heat we might remember.
Spring is far off when leaves unfold
Not duty bound to hurry,
Nor does snow's first flurry
Herald winter ice and cold
With crisp dryness in the air
And Jack Frost's patterns fair
Decorate window pane and screen,
His nip on extremities is keen.
What can this dismal month adorn
Save celebrate days we were born?

SENIOR CITIZEN

As the world spins on I feel left behind,
Out of touch; new technology surrounds,
Computers confuse keys to peruse
But labyrinthine procedures loose
Me, yet every possibility astounds.
Computers cannot memories find
Very doorways into my world,
(To what values would I now belong?)
Sights, experiences, people, places,
Vaguely remembered forgotten faces-
Might I get memories wrong?-
More visual than spoken is unfurled.
Is there Wisdom in my narrative
Or am I just a living archive?

Portrait Study.

TAKE ON RETIREMENT

When I retire is my garden heaven's door?
It's a time of change as I arrange
Flower beds around that earthen floor
When life's work for other projects I exchange.
I have time to watch plants grow
Painstakingly planted row by row
And seek to protect all those seeds
By declaring war on all those weeds.
Whether fruit and veg for the table
Or a border of flowers in fine display
All is nought when I am gone away
Unless continued by one more able
To tend this threshold of life beyond
Where paradise is never abandoned.

GRAVITY

> Celestial Thoughts a Mirror to Ourselves?

Encompassing force that keeps earth round
Despite stronger pressures locked within
Eludes scientists despite all they have found
To discover gravity's origin.
Its push equals not moon's pull on sea.
Other planets exert different degrees
Jumps on our moon would athletes please
Though they would breathless be.
Slingshot from other orbs propel
Spacecraft speed to greater galactic way.
Magnetism attracts or holds at bay
With invisible barrier like a spell
Reflecting mystery of human attraction;
Gravity mirrors a different connection.

BREXIT

If only we are allowed to fish
And from our own waters sell our catch
With fairer finances to match
We'd fix Brexit as we wish.
Soon the EU must face reality
By sorting out fiscal clarity.
We must be on the ball, no soft touch,
To utilize our own resources;
World Trade Org offers recourses
To better bargaining our selection
Than Europe's single market protection
Which we know costs far too much.
So fishermen, farmers, economists all
Rally round, prepare the shots to call.

GAME SHOOTING FOR THE POT

Flushed the high pheasant glides from tree top height
Testing if the gun below has shot with bite
Before curling either to left or right
While others from the roots with angled flight
Climb with whirring wings a double blur pale
Like fans on either side their barred long tail
Aiming for the sanctuary of kale
Further along the contoured dale.
Bright sunshine above the wood gives guns grief
Offering the saluted quarry some relief
Until down the line by swinging shot
One, other, both, even more are got.
The fortunes of gun 'gainst game wax and wane
Until the next drive all over again.

GREEDY GUNS, OR GREEDY SHOOTING LACKING GRACE.

Pheasants are good for a tasty meal
But can you eat 1,000 a week
Divided amongst shooting eights?
If game guns don't put on their plates,
When shot in quantity that satiates
Their dread desires with egos not meek,
Their greed for the kill kills the sport
Earning their behavior bad report.
(Fresh fare food banks cannot steal
For others that hunger alleviates.)
Birds in quantity are creatures still
Not mere targets for slaughtering skill.
WASTE NOT WANT NOT would go to halve
Numbers at home of those who starve.

> While I have enjoyed relaxed family days with friends with a pleasing but suitably modest bag I have witnessed the downside of guns elsewhere when working the dog.

BEETHOVEN & TS ELIOT QUARTETS.

Music's rhythms are sublime each time
I hear most composers' compositions:
Concertos, sonatas, symphonies mark,
Even instrumentations modern and stark,
Before we consider any vocal additions,
Integrated timing and variations.
Time is, was, will be, but once gone
Cannot be regained, instead a memory
Personal to each mind, unsharable
Movements with others unless able
To share the moment or story
Though their take won't be the same one.
Music echoes the poet's beat to scan
Who echoes in turn what musicians plan.

SYNCOPATED SOUND

Flappers, Chevrons & Homage to Vorticism.
Syncopated sound sunders all the rules
Sax machines breakdown notes, refine
Freeflow music of rhythm, and ragtime thrives
Reversing inhibitions, jazzing up lives,
Strident notes knocking convention, dress and design,
Simple, stark, grandly graphic; life cools
Such amalgam of culture. Postwar freedom
Upsets the usual routine, metallic, banjoed,
Chevroned, as diverse groupings strummed
For flappers in dance halls, tea time, frantically drummed
In architectural surroundings a la mode.
Block colour, this new age of jazz stirred the world
As black musicians played and sang couples furled.

MACBETH & AMBIGUITY

Macbeth the prisoner of his guilt
Sees how his visions have built
The evidence of his deeds to haunt
While tricks of the troubled mind taunt.
Ambition drives his wife to daunt
A rosier future by murder gaunt
Hands stained with innocent blood.
Like Saul before the witch of Endor
The crones cackle contradictory truth
Fountain of hideous wiles uncouth
When evil proves no defender
That from their actions comes no good.
They discover their fairest show
Mocks what their false hearts know.

Macbeth at Lady Margaret Hall.

LIVERY DINNERS

Self-important in inner city bubble
They eat their dinners speeches follow
Building liveried dullness
Socially measured no less
Convention bound somewhat hollow
But addressing some future trouble
Beyond the spectrum of finances.
Funding for good causes and charity
Is raised and wisely spent
Money given not lent
Monitored for clarity
Entrepreneurs' ideas enhances.
From such ritual and pomposity
There emerges measured generosity.

A PLACE OF PRAYER

Honi Soit Qui Mal Y Pense. St George's Chapel, Windsor.

Over stalls hang still the Garter banners
Heraldic helms topped with crazy crests
Punning the names of chosen knights.
The order founded to support regal claim
To foreign thrones or to think without shame
Of some lady's slipped garter minding manners.
Two dozen seem a tiny select corps
Though each might command soldiers by the score.
Edward's dream became a completed scheme.
Royal blue dominates in stained glass,
Roof bosses tell of Henry's knights past
Playing on each Companions' name;
Tall stalls support brass plates like frames
But jousting no longer dictates their games.

ON SUFFERING AND THE LORD'S PRAYER.

Job suffered all for what? God's glory
Comprises the assurance of our love
Tested to the time of trial to measure
Marking that our faith will assure
Our dependence on God, enthroned above,
Through the risen Christ, whose story
We accept, hoping to see him throned
On the right hand on high, spared
All delegated temptations,
The evil one's accusations.
Despite all suffering shared
Our tested loyalty is honed.
May thy kingdom come in whatever form
After we have weathered every storm.

DAWN, TRIUMPH OF LIGHT

The darkness is less dense becoming day
The impenetrable becomes shades of gray,
Softening as forms take gentle shape
Before dawn's crescendo and night's escape.
As streaks of orange and pinks
Fill the eastern sky – its umbra sinks.
Shadows take more solid form and pass
Lost to colour unweaved by light's loom,
No more obscure in a blanket of gloom,
Grisaille like medieval glass.
Day's inevitable triumph makes life less dense
Like strains of music break eerie silence.
Evening reverses stage by stage
The whole process like a mirror image.

THE TRUE VINEYARD, VINES AND VINEDRESSER.*

True vineyards harbour the community of vines
That the Father dresses through the Word made flesh,
Discarding the fruitless and pruning the rest
That whatever is yielded is only the best.
The true vineyard's abode keeps his vines fresh
Nurtured by the Word and his wonderful signs.
This is the vintage that filled ritual jars
Their abundance bringing joy, foretelling
Harmony in the marriage of Christ and believers,
The outflowing of heavenly grace like rivers,
Forgiving our sins which blemish and life mars.
Such solid stock is rooted in truth quelling
Within that rule of self to grow as it pleases
Which used to accuse destroys like fungal diseases.

* John 15.

ART & MODERNITY.

The artist creates by seeing, feeling, intuition
Maybe prompted by a word that leads not to fruition.
The mind's eye sees and conceives
The viewer may talk how their sense receives
Fruit of another discipline seen not read
Though established symbols may give a lead.
Expression free from constraint of time is addressed
Transcending ages though a commissioning church
May impose disciplines, discredit the artist's search
Where faith is measured, assessed, valued, expressed.
Fresh juxtaposition with Bible topics seen anew,
Balancing what is perceived a modern view.
Here are comments not made to fit
But there to prompt folk to think a bit.

A NOTE ON THE TYPE

The typeface used is Minion Pro derived from late Renaiassance classic typefaces by Adobe designer Robert Slimbach in 1990 to be versatile but clear enough for digital technology, yet flexible for a range of uses.

www.ingramcontent.com/pod-product-compliance
Lightning Source LLC
Chambersburg PA
CBHW050804160426
43192CB00010B/1638